Up 'n' Under

A play

John Godber

Samuel French - London
New York - Toronto - Hollywood

Please see page vi for further copyright information

UP 'N' UNDER

Up 'n' Under was given its world première by the Hull Truck Theatre Company at the Edinburgh Festival on 10th August 1984, where it won a Fringe First Edinburgh Festival Award. The cast was as follows:

Arthur Hoyle	Peter Geeves
Phil Hopley	Richard May
Frank Rowley	Richard Ridings
Tony Burtoft	Chris Walker
Steve Edwards ⎫ **Reg Welsh** ⎭	Andrew Dunn
Hazel Scott	Jane Clifford

Directed by John Godber

This production toured England and Scotland from September to December 1984, making a brief appearance at Hull Truck's home base, the Spring Street Theatre, Hull, and the Donmar Warehouse, London, following which it won the Laurence Olivier Award for Comedy of the Year, 1984.

Up 'n' Under transferred to the Fortune Theatre, London, on 26th March 1985. It was presented by Bill Kenwright with the following cast:

Arthur Hoyle	Stewart Howson
Phil Hopley	Richard James Lewis
Frank Rowley	Jonathan Linsley
Tony Burtoft	Chris Walker
Steve Edwards ⎫ **Reg Welsh** ⎭	Andrew Dunn
Hazel Scott	Sarah Harper

Directed by John Godber

COPYRIGHT INFORMATION

(See also page iv)

CHARACTERS

Arthur Hoyle: Ex-player. Owns a painting and decorating business
Phil Hopley: English teacher. An ex-Loughborough player
Frank Rowley: Local butcher
Tony Burtoft: Apprentice miner (striking)
Steve Edwards: Garage mechanic
Reg Welsh: Gambler and manager of the *Cobblers Arms*
Hazel Scott: Athlete and club-owner

The play may be presented without an interval if preferred

AUTHOR'S NOTE

The whole idea behind writing this play was to present a theme for the theatre in Hull. However, the story of the bet and the achievement of the men who accept the bet is universal ... thus the sundry references to the London Marathon as the absolute metaphor of amateur sport.

The staging needs to be fast and slick. The rugby sections that are apparent take into account that the dancer and not the poet is the father of the theatre. Thus this is an attempt to create a popular piece of drama that is all action—at the time of writing the most popular videos available on the mass market are the *Rocky* videos. This is an attempt to stage *Rocky* ... and where else? In Yorkshire, of course.

John Godber, 1984

To the Rugby League fans of Hull

ACT I

Frank, Hazel, Tony and Phil enter. They stand along the back. Frank takes a rugby shirt from the hooks and passes it across to Hazel. She catches it and places it carefully over the sit-ups rack. Frank takes up the speech

Frank Here on the very playing fields of Castleford your eyes will gaze in awe at splendid sights unseen . . . Your mind will jump and question the wisdom of our tale . . . But we care not. So, let battle cries be heard across our fair isle, from Hull . . . to Liverpool. Let trumpets sound and brass bands play their Hovis tunes.

Hazel throws the ball (which she has by now picked up from the bench) to Frank, then retreats back to her position UC

For here, upon this very stage, we see amateur Rugby League, a game born of rebellion, born of divide in eighteen ninety-five. For the working class of the North, for the working class. All around, pub teams throng the bars, club teams meet in lowly courts, amateurs all. Yet even as I speak a game commences in this battling competition; the *Crooked Billet* from Rochdale, play the *Cobblers Arms* from Castleford: unbeaten Gods of amateur Rugby sevens, unbeaten many seasons with greatness thrust upon them. Yet many know this to be true, still, one man takes the stage—our hero: Arthur Hoyle, a very lowly figure, yet the stature of a lion, a painter and decorator by trade. His quest will be within our two-hour traffic, to challenge the might of the Cobblers, to throw down the gauntlet and hope to break the myth that is the *Cobblers Arms* . . . His journey may be long and weary, and though you must travel with him, you never can assist, no matter how you pine to; your role is but to sit, and watch. Yet soft, for as you gaze upon our breezeblock "O" Reg Welsh appears, manager of the *Cobblers*, and trainer of their team; a very big fish on this our dish of amateur Rugby League. Here before your very eyes, two rivals meet: Reg and Arth.

Reg and Arthur enter

Reg Arthur.
Arthur Reg.
Frank And they will bet in lofty sums. But mark this, Arthur's coffers are very low, his mouth is very loose, and oft this and his brain are as separate as two mighty continents. My masters, is he mad or what is he? He is apt to make daft bets . . . to idle threats and boasts. From me enough, I let them play their stuff. So let our story now unfold, as two great rivals pledge their gold . . .
Reg Arthur . . .

Arthur Reg ...
Reg How are you, sunshine?
Arthur Not bad ...
Reg How's the wife?
Arthur Still living in the same house.
Reg Like that, is it, Arthur?
Arthur You know Doreen, Reg, she'd argue with fog.
Reg Takes after you, Arthur.
Arthur Dunno.
Reg No.
Arthur No, I've changed, Reg ... I was a hot-head, you know that as well as anybody ... I've cooled down.
Reg Good to hear that, Arth.
Arthur Well, old age and poverty helps, doesn't it?
Reg Dunno about the poverty.
Arthur No, right.
Reg You did some daft things in your day, Arthur lad.
Arthur I know.
Reg Can you remember when you poked the linesman in the eye at Warrington?
Arthur I can ...
Reg And when you head-butted the referee at St Helens?
Arthur Yeah.
Reg Eh, and when you burnt down the goal posts at 'unslett?
Arthur Oh, for disagreeing with that offside decision.
Reg Didn't see that one, read about it in the paper.
Arthur Good times, Reg.
Reg Yes.
Arthur Good times.
Reg I must say, Arthur ... it's good to see you settled.
Arthur Oh yeah ...
Reg The way you were going I never thought you'd make thirty ...
Arthur No ...
Reg You could still have been playing.
Arthur If it hadn't been for you, Reg ...
Reg Now don't be like that, Arth.
Arthur But it's true, you were on the board that got me banned, you know that as much as anybody.
Reg Let's not get in to all that ...
Arthur You brought it up.
Reg No matter what I say to you I'll not convince you that it wasn't only me who pushed to have you banned ... no matter what I say ...
Arthur That's the way I saw it, anyway ...

A beat

Reg Cigar?
Arthur Don't smoke.
Reg Still fit ... ?

Arthur Still trying ...

Reg Good to hear it.

Arthur We can't all live a life of leisure, can we Reg?

Reg But I've worked for it, Arthur sunshine ... worked for it ... making money is all about having money, investing money.

Arthur Yeah ...

Reg You must have a bob or two?

Arthur I've got a bob or two.

Reg I thought so ...

Arthur And that's all I've got.

Reg What do you think to my lads this year?

Arthur All right.

Reg Come on, Arthur ... they're more than all right, they're magnificent ... The Magnificent Seven, that's what I call them.

Arthur They've got their problems, Reg.

Reg What do you mean?

Arthur They're good on the ball ...

Reg Yeah ...

Arthur Bad in defence.

Reg Give over ... their defence is clam-tight ...

Arthur No, is it heck ...

Reg It is.

Arthur Well, you take it from me.

Reg The Cobblers'll beat any side you want to name.

Arthur They're not that good, Reg ... listen to me, I'm telling you.

Reg I thought you might have learnt some sense as times go on ... pity you haven't ... same old Arthur.

Arthur Same old Reg ... full of shit.

Reg Oh, you're not worth talking to.

Arthur The truth hurts.

Reg You make me laugh ... a feller with half an eye could see how good they are.

Arthur In that case I must be going blind.

Reg Look at that ... free and economic distribution ... fast hands ... unbeatable ... completely unbeatable.

Arthur No.

Reg They are.

Arthur Reg, they're not ...

Reg I'm not arguing with you ... you know I'm right.

Arthur I could train a team to beat 'em.

Reg Talk sense.

Arthur I'm talking sense.

Reg Doesn't sound much sense to me ...

Arthur I could get a team together to beat the Cobblers.

Reg Have you had some beer?

Arthur No ...

Reg Can you hear what you're saying?

Arthur I know what I'm saying and I mean it ... I've thought it for years.

Reg Arthur, you're talking out of your arsehole.

Arthur Steady.

Reg You are talking utter crap and you know it.

Arthur No, I'm not. I could get a team to beat 'em.

Reg Don't be such a pillock.

Arthur I said steady with the language, Reg.

Reg Well, you're talking such rubbish, man.

Arthur I'm not talking rubbish, I'm talking facts ... there's a way to beat these, no problem.

Reg There's no way you're gonna get an amateur club to beat these, no way.

Arthur Rubbish.

Reg No way.

Arthur Rubbish.

Reg No way, Arthur ...

Arthur I could do it ... I could train any team in the North to beat these.

Reg OK then, put your money where your mouth is.

Arthur Eh ... ?

Reg Put your money where your mouth is ...

Arthur Ar ... dunno ...

Reg See what I mean ... You're the one who's full of shit.

Arthur All right, then, I bet you ...

Reg That you can train a given team to beat my lads?

Arthur Yeah, I bet you, Reg.

Reg How much? Four grand ... five thousand ... ten thousand, Arthur? Let's make it a decent bet, shall we?

Arthur I bet my mortgage ...

Reg What about Doreen?

Arthur I bet my house ...

Reg Keep it sensible ...

Arthur I bet my house that I can get a team to beat them set of nancy poofters, Reg Welsh ... that's the bet, shake on it ...

Reg You'll lose ...

Arthur We'll see ...

Reg I mean it.

Arthur Any team in the North, come on, name a club side ... I'll train 'em.

Reg We'll meet in the next sevens.

Arthur When is it?

Reg Five weeks' time ...

Arthur That's great ... name my name.

Reg No turning back ...

Arthur You've got my word ...

Reg It's a bet?

Arthur Come on, name the team I've got to train.

Reg I'll make arrangements for us to meet in the draw.

Arthur I'll leave the dirty work to you.

Reg I'll pull a few influential strings.

Arthur What's the team, Reg ... ?

Reg I name the Wheatsheaf from near Hull.
Arthur Nice one ... now name a team.
Reg I name the Wheatsheaf, Arthur.
Arthur The *Wheatsheaf Arms*?
Reg That's the one.
Arthur You're joking.
Reg The bet's on ...
Arthur Bloody hell ...
Reg Five weeks then, Arthur ... I look forward to the game ...

Reg exits

Arthur The *Wheatsheaf*?

Arthur exits

Hazel Now, hear this news of the *Wheatsheaf* ... The *Wheatsheaf Pub* ... infamous in rugby circles. Yet in all their history they have never won a single game, and what's the same, they never have seven men. As you saw, Arthur's head was loose, he wished he'd shut his gob. You know right well the bet is unfair, but to pull out now would be disaster. The path he treads is narrow and long ... the job is on ... to train this team into the likes of which has ne'er been seen.

Hazel exits

The Lights come up on Frank, Tony and Phil, who are sitting despondently in their dressing-room

Frank Give 'em another five minutes ... then ... home ...
Phil There is a brighter side to it, historically speaking.
Tony What?
Phil The long-running tradition of the Wheatsheaf team losing, because of lack of players.
Tony I wonder what's happened to Steve and Tommy?
Frank Steve'll be messing about with his car putting new headlights on it ... or cleaning the engine down with Palmolive.
Tony It's a smart car he's got ... goes like a bomb.
Frank It ought to go like a bomb and blow his bloody head off.
Phil Sick jokes ...
Frank Thank you, doctor.
Tony Well, anyway, this is my last game.
Phil And me ... the last time I'm going to look a prat.
Tony If we can't get seven then that's it for me, anyway, you don't look a prat.

Phil notices Tony has no socks

Phil Where's your socks?
Tony Forgotten 'em.
Phil Brilliant!
Tony I can't afford to be going out and buying sock after sock ...

Phil That's brilliant, that is, there's only three of us, and you two look pathetic. You could at least make an effort.

Frank We have made an effort, we've turned up.

Phil You're not playing in them, are you?

Frank What?

Phil Jesus sandals ...

Frank Why not?

Tony What if somebody stamps on your toe?

Frank I'll crucify 'em.

Tony Sandals, that's just the pits, that is ...

Frank I'm playing in these and you lot can knackers.

Phil Oh, I mean, this is just pathetic ... we can't play with three ...

Tony Maybe we could ask to borrow a couple on loan for half an hour.

Frank Yeah, a couple of props from the Cobblers.

Tony If we run about really fast maybe they'll think there's more.

Frank Yeah ...

Tony I was joking.

Frank It's a bit desperate, really.

Phil Did either of you train this week?

Tony What was that?

Phil Train ... you know training ...

Frank Is that a foreign ... ?

Phil Try saying it ... it's dead easy ... training ...

Frank Is it French?

Tony Tra—track ...

Phil No ... training ...

Tony Pain ... paining ...

Phil Nearly.

Tony No, I can't say it.

Frank I can't do it ... the last time I trained, Queen Victoria had just died.

Tony Last time I trained she'd just been born.

Phil The last time I trained the earth was a gaseous mass.

Tony Weird ...

Steve appears

Steve ... yo ...

Frank Yo ... Steve ...

Phil Yo ...

Steve Yo ... here we go, here we go, here we go ...

Phil Where's the others?

Tony Where've you been?

Steve Got lost in Goole ... found this great pub ... Theakston's Old Peculiar on draft ...

Tony Nice one.

Phil Where's Tommy and Jack?

Steve Tommy can't come and Jack's wife says he's gone fishing.

Phil Brilliant!

Frank Why can't Tommy make it?

Steve I think him and their lass have had a bit of an argument. I could hear her shouting as I walked down the garden so I thought I'd leave it.

Phil Oh brilliant thinking, Steve ... if you'd've called for him he might have come.

Tony If you say brilliant again I'll die.

Phil Brilliant.

Steve We're not going to play with just four, are we?

Frank Are you joking ... ? We were playing with three.

Steve Let's leave it and get in the beer tent ...

Frank Get changed, it'll be a laugh.

Steve Who for?

Tony Upton Social Club and about a hundred and fifty spectators.

Frank Look at it like this, if we lose it's only fifteen minutes then straight into the beer tent.

Steve Hey, I don't like all this positive talk.

Tony Like what?

Steve Like *if* we lose ... I'm more used to *when* we lose.

Phil At least it's not raining ...

Tony There's a bad wind, though ...

Steve There's a bad wind in here. Is it you?

Tony Is it heck.

Frank It's that Theakston's.

Steve is looking in his bag

Steve Oh shite, man ... I've left me shirt ...

Phil Oh thanks ... that's ...

Tony Bloody brilliant ...

Frank I've got a spare one ... (*He dips into his bag and produces a massive shirt*) Here, get that on ...

Steve Oh, I can't wear that, Frank ... I'll look like a balloon.

Tony Get it on ... bit of wind and you'll be laughing.

Phil Put a shirt on, Steve, I feel sick.

Steve Shut your moustache, will you?

Frank Come here, let me play a tune on your ribs.

Steve puts the shirt on

Steve Look at this.

Phil Man at Top Shop?

Tony Wham! Jitterbug.

Frank Man at Oxfam.

Tony Who does the shirt belong to, Frank? Your lass?

A beat

Phil Oh, sore point.

Frank That's the only bloody thing she left when she went.

Steve Have you got a mortgage for it?

Frank I've got some good memories of that shirt ... we useter go camping in it.

Phil Right, are we ready! Steve, ready?

Steve has the shirt on but is looking for his jockstrap in his bag

Steve That's not mine . . .
Tony Well, it's not mine . . .
Phil Come on, let's start to think about the game.
Tony Rugby is a game played by men with odd-shaped balls.
Frank Oh, oh . . . every one a winner. For me rugby is a game of two halves.
Tony Give blood: play rugby.
Frank Give orange: play squash.

Tony groans

Hey, not bad, I just made that up.
Phil Right, listen . . . are we going to play or not?
Steve No.
Tony Might as well . . .
Frank We can ask to put one man in the scrum.
Steve We're not going to do the war-chant, are we?

They perform a hideous war-chant

Phil Are we hell, let's just get out there . . . and get it bloody over with.
Steve Let's get in that bloody beer tent.

They all run downstage and find a space. The weather is quite cold and they react accordingly. Steve will tuck his hands right down his shorts. Tony has picked up the ball

Tony Tony Burtoft. Apprentice miner. Age twenty-two. Weight one hundred and ninety pounds. Height six point one. Position Centre. Hobbies: racing whippets.

The ball is thrown

Frank Frank Rowley. Butcher. Age thirty-two. Weight two hundred and fifteen pounds. Height six point one. Position Prop. Hobbies: anything to do with my hands.

The ball is thrown

Steve Steve Edwards. Car Mechanic. Age twenty-five. Weight one hundred and eighty pounds. Height six point one. Position Loose Forward. Hobbies: drinking.

The ball is thrown

Phil Phil Hopley. Teacher. Age twenty-nine. Weight one hundred and sixty pounds. Height five point eight. Position Stand-off. Hobbies: reading, Scrabble, hunting around antique fairs on a Sunday.

Pause

Right, here we go . . . if anyone gets the ball, this time . . . pass!
All Oh yeah . . .

The players go upstage and freeze

Hazel enters

Hazel   I' faith, good sirs, the fools the Wheatsheaf played
              And lost well bad
              The largest defeat they'd ever had.
              The petal-soft warriors sickened by the score,
              Will in time vow to play no more
              Take heed of how they've lost a game,
              I' faith, good sirs, who can they blame . . . ?
              Only themselves . . .
              Thus Arthur's quest is harder still,
              Made so by our author's quill . . .
              How can they play with motive gone . . . ?
              Can Arthur coax them . . . ?
              Now watch on . . .

Hazel exits

The players come out of their freeze. Phil leaves the ball upstage

Phil That is it this time and I mean it . . .
Steve And me . . .
Phil You? You never did a bloody thing.
Steve Why, what did you do?
Phil At least I moved.
Tony Did you? I must have blinked.
Phil Why don't you tackle, Steve?
Steve Why don't you pass?
Phil I did pass.
Steve Not to me . . .
Phil I can't pass to you unless you move on to the ball . . . and don't stand
  there like a dickhead.
Frank I think I'll have a nice big piece of T-bone when I get home . . .
Tony I bet we'd beat 'em at darts.
Steve Dominoes.
Frank Drinking . . . (*He laughs*)

Arthur enters upstage and crouches down to the players

Arthur All right, fellers?
Tony ⎱ (*together*) All right.
Steve ⎰
Arthur Arthur . . . Arthur Hoyle nice to meet you.
Phil Don't tell me you're a scout for the British touring party.
Frank Don't you mean ENSA?
Arthur No . . . I thought you had a bit of bad luck in that game . . .

They all burst out laughing

Steve Hey, come on, man, fifty-four–nil in fifteen minutes, that's more than
  a bit of bad luck.

Tony That's a tragedy.

Arthur You can laugh but I thought you displayed some fine talent, some promise.

Tony Has he got a white stick?

Frank Has he got a brain?

Arthur OK, there were only four of you . . . but even so.

Phil Yeah, well, thanks for the thoughts.

Arthur Do you have a trainer?

Steve Do worms have legs?

Frank We did . . . but he's gone fishing.

Arthur Look . . . I don't know how you'd feel about this, but I'd be willing to train you . . . help you out . . . I used to play a bit.

Phil No . . . er . . .

Arthur I tell you what we could do if you like . . . Give me a trial . . . Five weeks' trial . . . How about that? Just up to the next sevens.

Phil No thanks, mate . . .

Steve Hang on, Phil. How do we know that you're any good?

Arthur That's why I'm suggesting that you take me on for a five-week trial.

Frank Well, it's not for me, I've had enough.

Arthur Come on fellers, you don't mean to tell me that you're willing to pack in playing rugby as easy as that?

Frank Yeah, that's exactly what I mean.

Steve We can't even muster seven players.

Arthur That's where I come in . . . use my influence . . . pull a few strings . . .

Frank No . . . we're over the bloody hill.

Arthur (*aside*) I'll rot in hell for the lies I tell. (*To the players*) Rubbish, over the hill . . . Look at Brian Bevan.

Frank It's too much like hard work.

Steve Yeah . . . thanks anyway.

Arthur Oh, come on lads . . . give us a break.

Tony What's in it for you?

Arthur Love of the game, that's all . . .

Phil I don't know . . .

Arthur Listen, come to training at Walton sports fields . . . Tuesday, right? Think about it.

Phil Yeah, we will.

Steve I'm gonna think about that beer tent.

Frank Mmmm, nice idea . . .

Steve, Phil and Frank stand to leave

Steve See you, Arthur, nice to meet yer . . .

They start to walk off

Arthur Think about Tuesday, lads.

They give a disinterested "yeah" and exit

Tony remains. A beat

Good lads.
Tony Not bad.
Arthur Lost interest?
Tony Yeah ... Winning's easy, innit? Losing's hard.
Arthur Don't tell me. How long have you been playing? (*He throws the ball to Tony*)
Tony Oh, a ball! Started at school.
Arthur Haven't you got any proper kit?
Tony Nobody's bothered ... We useter pay subs but that's died off. Did you see Frank's sandals ... ? He's daft. Apparently he was a right animal ... but their lass left home and he lost interest.
Arthur Self-respect?
Tony What?
Arthur Don't matter ... What about the others?
Tony Phil's a decent player when he gets the right ball ... He's a play-maker ... he played at College or summat in Leicester ... summat.
Arthur Loughborough?
Tony Yeah, I think that's it. Rugby Union.
Arthur Ay, it would be ... whisper it.
Tony Yeah.

A beat

Did you play?
Arthur Hey, I'm not that old.
Tony Er ...
Arthur Hooker ... Wakey Trinity.
Tony Whoooohhhh!
Arthur I played a couple of first-team games.
Tony Got the build for a hooker.
Arthur Yeah ... What's happened to the other three?
Tony Hardly ever turn up.
Arthur Haven't you got any influence?
Tony No way.
Arthur You could have a word with them couldn't you ... ? Get them to train.
Tony I can try, but I can't promise ...
Arthur I'll give you a couple of quid ...
Tony What?
Arthur If you have a word ...
Tony Yeah, can do.
Arthur Look, here's a fiver ... just have a word with 'em, get 'em out there on Tuesday ...
Tony What's it all about, this?
Arthur I love the game, that's all, let's just say that.
Tony You can say what you like for a fiver.
Arthur You'll train, won't you?
Tony Yeah.
Arthur What do you think to the *Cobblers Arms*?

Music

Tony Brilliant.
Arthur Do you think so?
Tony There's not a team in the North to touch 'em ... unbeatable ...
Arthur I don't know. How would you feel about playing against 'em?
Tony They're in a different league, man, it'd be like playing against tanks.

The music fades

Arthur Anyway, it's only a thought ... We can dream, can't we?
Tony Dream we can.
Arthur Do what you will, you know, Tuesday?
Tony Yeah, right, I'll get off, then ... see you ...
Arthur Tuesday.

Tony exits

Our lass'll kill me ...

Black-out

She'll kill me.

Reg enters behind Arthur

Reg I'm not a wicked man, though many say I am a bastard. I'm a fair man, I like to see fair play. Old Arthur's sweating, I can smell his pig-like stench from here. Silly sod to bet his house in such a way, and as you saw I tried to speak in sensible terms and halt his foolish gob. I wouldn't take a house, not from an ordinary bloke. I wouldn't let him choke by Doreen's hand. Here's what I'll do: I'll conjure a note, and on it I've wrote: "It's a determined man who's bet all he's got." I'll take three grand off you in this bet, Arthur, pal. Don't want to see a proud man out of house and home.
Arthur Three grand, Reg.
Reg In cash, I like cash. What the hell would I do with your hovel, anyway?
Arthur Yeah, right, thanks Reg.
Reg How's the training going, Arthur?
Arthur Great.
Reg Yeah?
Arthur Couldn't be better.
Reg Lads eager, are they?
Arthur Yeah ... As soon as I put the prospect to them they almost bit my hand off.
Reg Really?
Arthur Have you made enquiries about the draw?
Reg You leave that to me ... I'm even thinking of giving you a bye to the final ... Make it more of a prestige game for your lads ... Don't want to leave 'em with nothing.
Arthur Yeah ... right ...
Reg Just make sure that you've got a team ... otherwise it could be embarrassing.

The Light goes out on Reg, who exits

Arthur takes off his anorak through the ensuing speech. He wears a rugby shirt under his coat. A rugby ball is thrown on to him. He looks around for the players to appear

Arthur Tuesday night I waited and waited ... Walton sports field was a desert of green, with not a player to be seen at all ...

Hazel enters and sits on a bench

Hazel   My Lords, on Waltons fields he stood in storms and hail,
                   And blowing gales the like of which would crack your
                        cheeks,
                   Which you have heard from tales.
                   Every hour he stood alone the stronger grew his cause,
                   More determined was his soaking gait.
                   But still his part was to wait ... and wait ...
                   His thoughts lay with success,
                   He knew he dare not fail ...
                   And as he stood drenched on yon fair fields ...
                   The rest were supping ale ...

Downstage are Frank and Phil, with a drink of beer. They have had a few

Phil Oh funny ... honestly funny ... some of the things they come out with, honestly funny.
Frank Yeah?
Phil Oh yeah ...
Frank Like what?
Phil Oh, all sorts ... I mean, stories in the staff-room, funny.
Frank Yeah, yeah ... like what?
Phil Like this kid writes, William the Conqueror's first name was Norman.

This meets with death

Frank (*taking a drink*) Oh yeah.
Phil (*undaunted*) Funny ... and this lad says ... No, I can't tell you, it's sick.
Frank Tell us, Phil man.
Phil No, it'll upset you, it's sick ... you're a man of sensibilities, you're a sensitive man, Frank ...
Frank I cut dead meat up ... I'd hardly call that sensitive.
Phil So ... I've got this class ... a couple of years ago ... and this has just come to me ... we're talking about the Ripper ...
Frank Yeah ... yeah ...
Phil A slow-learning group ... reading and writing problems ...
Frank Like me ...
Phil And we're trying to diagnose what to do with the Yorkshire Ripper.
Frank Yeah, go on ...
Phil And this little lad says ... "Sir?"
Frank Yeah ...

Phil "Sir, I know what we could do with the Yorkshire Ripper" . . . I says, "Great, go on, Stuart . . . what would you do?" Then he says . . . "I'd send him to America."

Frank (*beginning to laugh*) Norman the Conqueror . . .

Frank and Phil begin to cackle and then the cackling subsides. They both sigh . . . drink their beer

Black-out on Frank and Phil. A Light on Arthur

Arthur And I'm waiting and waiting.

The Lights come up on Frank and Phil

Phil What do you think to this Arthur bloke?

Frank He's got a painting and decorating firm, I've seen his van . . . Decent player in his day.

Phil Could be handy, could that . . . I want my living-room Artexing.

Frank What do you reckon about *this* lot . . . ?

Phil I don't know . . .

Frank He's keen . . .

Phil If he's out on Walton sports field by himself he is keen. He'll be arrested for loitering.

Frank Wonder who turned up?

Phil I could guess . . .

Frank Not Steve . . .

Phil No chance . . . he'll be trying to pick something up.

Frank He ought to pick something up, incurable.

Phil Tony'll turn out.

Frank Yeah . . . mate I was talking to yesterday reckons this Arthur's a weird bloke . . . says his brain's in a box somewhere.

Phil Yeah?

Frank Hard case.

Phil Just let him start with me.

Frank And me . . .

Phil I'll tell him where to get off . . . Listen, you couldn't see your way to letting me have another batch of them T-bones, could you? You know those you got off the back of a warehouse?

Frank Yeah, come and pick them up . . . and bring a few mags with you . . .

Phil You dirty sod.

Frank Where do you get them from?

Phil All over the place, you never know when they're gonna show up. The other day we were reading *Women in Love*, this fifth-year lad whips out this porno book. "Look at this, sir," he says. "This is women in love" . . . I'd never seen anything like it . . . I gave him a dressing-down, made him feel embarrassed and confiscated the magazine, told him I was going to burn it.

Frank And did you?

Phil Did I hell . . . I kept it . . . it was a classic . . . I'll bring it down.

Frank If you would . . . Another drink?

Phil How many's this?

Frank This is six ...
Phil Yeah, go on, then, I haven't got far to walk ...
Frank No?
Phil No, only to the car ... (*He drinks and hands Frank his glass*) Cheers.

Black-out. A light on Hazel

Hazel Yet still alone, and with his thoughts only, he sat there bald and wet, and yet the wind and rain had ceased and all the air was clear ... He turned his mind to lofty thoughts of subjects he held dear.

A Light comes up on Arthur

Arthur This never happens in *Rocky* ... I love *Rocky*, me. I've seen them all, *Rocky One*, *Two* and *Three*. I like *Rocky Two* the best, you know where Adrian's dying in hospital and Rocky's there with his trainer, and she just moves her fingers and says, "Win, Rocky, win". Oh, I was just stood in the cinema, shouting. I felt a right fart, and when I looked around everybody else was shouting and all.

The Light goes out on Arthur

Hazel And so the time has come and on this stage, good sirs, needs must I play my part, and meet our hero face to face. The sands of time run fast ... five weeks is but a blink in the history of our globe. Arthur's quest is waning and Reg has his team in training. (*Hazel drops into a press-up position and begins to perform press-ups with ease*)
Arthur Not bad ...
Hazel Eh?
Arthur Pretty impressive.
Hazel If you're a flasher, I'm not interested.
Arthur You what?
Hazel If you're one of those little men who hangs about flashing his wares, I'm not interested.
Arthur I'm not a flasher ... I'm training ...
Hazel Training ... ugh?
Arthur My lads are on a five-mile run ... (*Aside*) I'll rot in hell for the lies I tell.
Hazel And you're the first one back?
Arthur Sharp ... very sharp ...
Hazel Oh, trainer eh ... ? I didn't realize.
Arthur Been jogging, have you?
Hazel Yeah. Light jog ... I've just had a heavy session.
Arthur Husband at home, then, is he ... ?
Hazel Don't come the crudity with me fatty, you're barking up the wrong tree.
Arthur Oh, I stand corrected.
Hazel Weights ... I train with weights ...
Arthur A couple of bags of sugar on the end of a broomhandle?
Hazel Oh, I can see that you're fit ... every curve in your physique screams out ... fitness ... How often do you train—once a year?

Arthur Ha ha ... very funny ...

Hazel You men make me laugh ...

Arthur That's hard ... I bet ... seeing you ...

Hazel I see them like you down at the club, a game of squash, a sauna, twenty cigs, and a heart attack ... Rugby players are the worst. Training session and then seven pints of Guinness ... Fitness ... you don't know what fitness is ...

Arthur Here, catch ...

Arthur throws the ball quite hard but she catches it easily. Through this speech they continue to pass the ball

Where's this club, then?

Hazel Above the supermarket.

Arthur Oh yeah ...

Hazel Showers ... sauna ... solarium, loose weights ... getting some Nautilus at Christmas.

Arthur How much is it, then?

Hazel Interested, are you?

Arthur Only making conversation ...

Hazel You could have a free trial.

Arthur Who owns it?

Hazel A woman called Hazel Scott ...

Arthur Dave Scott's wife ... the international scrum half ...

Hazel That's right ... we separated two years ago ... Give me a ring if you're interested ... we're in the Yellow Pages ... I'll show you what training is ...

Arthur I doubt it ...

Hazel If I was you, I'd start to worry about your team ... I think they must have got lost ...

Arthur Now I can see why your husband left you ...

Hazel I left him ...

Hazel exits, taking the ball with her. She reaches a side of the stage and does a perfect reverse pass

Arthur catches it ... and follows her off

Arthur Not bad ... hey, listen ...

Arthur exits

The Lights go down, then come up again

Steve comes on, wearing a pair of overalls. He lies down and is looking under a car. Phil follows, wearing a track suit, and then Frank, in his butcher's togs. Their speeches overlap, and their actions are done to the audience

Steve I think that what you've got is a fracture on a brake pipe ... fluids escaping, and you need new shock absorbers on both the front sides. Apart from that, and a dicky front light, the car's fine.

Phil The kestrel is, of course, not only a real feature in Casper's life, but it also serves as a symbol of the freedom that Casper will never have himself until he manages to escape from the environment that he currently finds himself caged in.

Frank I can't really let you have that for less than two pound. It's best rump steak, you see . . . I've got to make a living. Tell you what . . . give us one-ninety.

Arthur enters upstage

Arthur Oi!

All Sorry, what did you say . . . Sir?/Lad?/Love?

Arthur Oi, it's me . . .

They all look around for Arthur, who has invaded their very privacy

All What?

Arthur What happened . . . ?

All What?

Arthur What happened on Tuesday, lads, eh?

All Not here, I'm busy . . .

Arthur I said . . . what bloody happened?

All (*whispering*) Go away.

Arthur No.

All Look, this is very embarrassing . . . sorry . . . Sir/Class/Love . . .

Arthur Come tomorrow . . . Walton fields . . .

All Go away . . .

Arthur Tomorrow?

All All right . . .

Arthur See you tomorrow, then . . .

Arthur goes. General cover lights

Phil   Now soon to sing their songs of old,
                  Their battle chants of war,
                  So let music play and voices swell
                  And sunken hearts rise from dark hell.

Steve, Frank and Phil take off their outer clothes, revealing training gear, tracksuits, etc.

Hey, Frank . . . "She was poor but she was honest." (*He sings*) "She was poor but she was honest . . . Victim of a rich man's whim . . ."

All (*singing*)   First he ****** her, then he left her,
                    And she had a child by him.
                    It's the same the whole world over . . .
                    It's the poor what gets the blame . . .
                    It's the rich what gets the pleasure
                    And it's all the bloody same . . .

Tony enters, in training gear

Steve Hey up . . . Club song . . . "Blackbird" . . .

Frank Which version . . . clean or filthy . . . ?
Tony Filthy . . .
Phil You lot are worse than the kids at school.
Tony We are kids . . .
Steve Some of us . . .
Tony Ooohh, getting all defensive, just because you shave . . . don't come all macho . . .
Steve Oh big word for an apprentice miner i'n't?
Tony Here's another big word . . .
Steve What?
Tony Eat shit, you skinny gett!
Frank I love the humour . . .
Steve "Blackbird" . . . Club song by Steve Edwards . . . Mr Hopley, sir . . .
Phil Is it one of your own compositions, lad?
Steve Yes sir . . . It's taken me years of creative turmoil and anguish . . .
Phil Right, let's hear it, lad, if it's any good you can put it in your sixteen-plus English file . . .

Steve   Once a boy was no good . . . took a girl into a wood . . .
Frank   Bye bye blackbird . . .
Steve   Laid her down upon the grass . . .
                 Pinched her tits and slapped her arse . . .
All   Bye bye blackbird . . .
Steve   Took her where nobody else could find her . . .
                 To a place where he could really grind her . . .
                 Rolled her over on her front . . .
                 Shoved his . . .
All   Yo . . .
Steve   Right up her . . .
All   Ears . . . Blackbird bye bye . . .

Phil Give me the other version, any day . . .
Steve Boring . . .
Frank Three out of ten . . .
Tony One out of twenty from the Russian judge . . .
Phil (*in a French accent*) Luxembourg . . . nil points . . .
Tony Get this one going . . . ba da da . . . ba da da . . .

They do a rendition of the Flying Pickets: "Spring in the Air" . . . It is a common impersonation of the Flying Pickets

> *As they sing, Arthur enters with a number of rugby balls under his arms. He throws the balls to the lads*

Arthur Catch . . . What have we got here, "Opportunity Knocks"?
Frank Just having a song . . .
Arthur If you want to sing, you're in the wrong game . . .
Phil Just a laugh . . .
Arthur Just . . . let's have a word . . . I don't want to waste time. Tonight we'll work on general fitness . . . cardiovascularity.
Steve I think my tea's ready . . .
Tony Shurrup.

Steve Don't start ...

Arthur Ball-handling ... and the speed of moving the ball from the ... play the ball ...

Phil We know all this ...

Arthur I'm assuming you know nothing ...

Tony He doesn't ...

Phil Piss off ...

Tony Touchy ...

Arthur I want to know if you've ever had any set moves, from penalties ... or from scrumming ...

Phil What about other players ... ?

Arthur That's my worry ... I'll be playing hooker for a start ...

Steve Can you hook?

Arthur You'll have to wait and see ...

Tony What time'll we finish?

Arthur Why?

Steve He's got to be in bed ...

Frank With their lass ...

Tony I don't want to be late ...

Frank Nor me ...

Arthur Look, let's just make a start ... Right ... let's have a run.

Frank A what?

Arthur Start off with three miles ... just to get warm.

Steve Warm ... ?

Frank No ... I'm not running about ... I've been on my feet all day at work ... I'll have a game of touch and pass ...

Arthur It's only a short run, Frank.

Frank I don't want to overdo it, I want to be able to walk tomorrow.

Phil Come on Frank ... take it steady ...

Arthur Look, it's not a race ... it's just a matter of finishing ... Don't you watch the London Marathon?

Frank Watch, yeah ...

Tony Let's get summat done ... I'm gonna miss "Top of the Pops" at this rate ...

Frank Oh, come on, then ...

They all stand in a line across the stage. Those not talking make a heavy breathing and plodding noise ... (sub-Berkoff)

Steve Out we went ... over the crisp grass of Waltons fields ... Down the slope which led to the main road ...

Phil Through the gate ... and on to the pavement ...

Tony The change of running surface ... jarred ...

Steve Arthur led ...

Frank And we like warriors followed bunched behind him ...

Steve The night was drawing in ...

Arthur It wasn't dark but ... it would be in the hour ...

Phil Car side lights were beginning to ease their way effortlessly towards us ...

Tony Sodium street lights sparkled to life ...

Steve As we hit a hump-backed bridge ... the weariness ... the fatigue ...

Phil The complete and utter lack of fitness was beginning to register in us all ...

Steve My legs felt heavy ... calves aching ... a hard pounding drumming reverberating up my back ...

Tony The bridge brow was in sight and then the descent ...

Frank Twenty yards of easy running ...

Arthur I didn't realize that three miles was so long ...

Frank Saliva dripping from my mouth like a hungry dog ... and I was aware of the effort of moving my frame ...

Steve The dread of meeting pedestrians loomed ...

Phil And mannequins ... grinning, smirking their smug sickly expressions ...

Steve Their form is constant ...

Frank They never change ... age leaves them untouched ...

Tony Our tracks rumbled along the tarmac ...

Phil The sight of people ... and the impulse to make more effort to push harder ...

Arthur Fifty-five minutes ... for three miles a slow pace ... but a lot of meat in the pack ... we returned with the light fading ...

They are all exhausted and collapse where they are

Get your breath ... All right, Frank ... ?

Frank Just about ... feel a bit sick ...

Frank Deep breaths, Frank son ...

Frank I'm OK ...

Steve Nice one, Frankie ...

Frank I bet I can't move tomorrow ...

Arthur You will ... same again tomorrow ...

Phil What next, Arthur?

Frank That'll do for me ...

Phil Not bad for a start. I'm about as fit as D. H. Lawrence.

Arthur I think he's dead.

Phil That's what I mean.

Steve Nice and easy session ... pass me the Guinness drip, will you ... ?

Tony Enjoyed it ...

Steve I have.

Phil You're not a bad bloke, are you Arthur?

Arthur Aren't I?

Phil No, you're all right, mate, all right ... I had my doubts ... but you're an honest man ... I can smell a crook, but you're OK ...

Arthur Thanks ...

Phil I mean it ...

Tony Yeah ... and me ...

Frank Do you know what our training amounted to in the past? We'd meet in the *Wheatsheaf* ... have about six pints, pick thirteen men ...

Steve If thirteen ever turned up ...

Frank Then it was back to my place to watch the videos ...
Arthur I love *Rocky* ... *One, Two* and *Three* ...
Phil Pulp crap ...
Arthur Oh, Barry friggin' Normans now, are we ... ?
Steve Hey, we had some laughs. Can you remember that time when Jack's
   cousin said that he wanted a game ... turned up, played and got his ear-
   lobe bit off.
Frank He played well ...
Phil We only lost thirty–nil that game.
Arthur No more losing talk ... think positive. I want to succeed.
Tony I know what'll succeed: a budgie with no teeth.
Phil That's the sort of comment this team doesn't need.
Steve Let's not get into it tonight, eh?
Frank Yeah ...
Steve Can you remember when I broke my hand?
Tony You didn't do that playing rugby.
Phil That's true.
Steve I'll tell you what I did do. I shat into my shorts once.

Black-out. They freeze. Arthur stands behind them in overhead light

Arthur Ar ... you're good lads, honest, no edge to you ... you love
   needling each other. The only thing you have in common is the game ... I
   feel a right prat, you've taken to me, and you don't know why I'm doing
   all this. In any case I don't think about it much ... only at nights ... I lay
   awake ...

The Lights come up

Steve Get away man ... I don't believe you.
Phil It's true, and she married his brother-in-law's nephew ...
Frank What did Jack say?
Phil What would you say ... ?
Steve She looks like a really nice lass and all.
Arthur I tell you what ... let's get down to the *Wheatsheaf* and have a pint,
   shall we?
Tony Sounds like a good idea.
Steve That's the sort of training I like Arthur.
Phil What about the fitness ... ?
Arthur Look at it like this ... it's a celebration ... all I want to do is to show
   my gratitude to you lot for turning out for training.
Frank You had to twist our arms a bit, though.
Phil I nearly had a fit when you came into school, the kids went wild ...
Arthur I think it's the head ...
Phil Probably ...
Arthur Well, what do you say, then ... ? A swift five down the *Wheatsheaf
   Arms*? I'll get the first round in.
Steve I'll drink to that ...
Frank And me ...

A change of lighting. The players set up the gymnasium with the following equipment: lat machine, exercise bike, bench press, hack-squat, sit-ups bench, step-up bench

> *Steve exits*

> *Hazel enters*

Hazel And so to play a major part within this vasty "O". Arthur trained with just one jog, his players' skills, well, naff, he could have laughed but took them for a drink of sack. Now remember how on Walton fields came the offer of a club. It was training that would win the day, not supping in the pub. Thus Hazel takes the boards once more, training in her gym, all plush and modern and well equipped; well fit athletes train, and gross obese men slim. But soft . . .

The players chuckle with glee

> For as we speak, the tissue paper gladiators approach, led by their hero our coach. How will they fair with yon weights? The training will be tough. I see a question on yon fair face, sirs, are they man enough? (*She proceeds to the sit-ups bench and begins exercising*)

The players have frozen at the back of the stage

Tony Hey, not bad.
Frank Nice work.
Phil Arthur, who's that?
Arthur Ar, right. Hazel, can I introduce you to the team . . . ?
Hazel Yeah.
Arthur This is Tony, Phil, Frank.
Hazel Hallo. Come to have a go at getting fit, have you?
Tony Yeah.
Hazel How are the ten-mile runs?
Frank What?
Arthur Great, thanks.
Hazel It's going to be hard slog . . . over the next twelve sessions.
Tony Yeah . . .
Phil Be gentle with us . . .
Hazel (*to the audience*) I took them around each machine, explaining its function and explaining some common fallacies about weight-training. I could see at a glance that they were sceptical, to say the least.

Phil is on the exercise bike

Phil (*whispering*) She's not training us, is she?
Arthur In a word?
Phil In a word . . .
Arthur Yes.
Frank Great stuff.
Phil You're joking.
Tony He is.

Arthur I'm not ...
Phil She's a woman ...
Arthur I thought you were educated ...
Phil I am ...
Arthur She's probably twice as fit as you ...
Tony No way ...
Arthur Just give it a go ...
Frank I'm not bothered ... It's a good idea.
Phil I'll just feel uncomfortable ...
Arthur She's useter training men ...
Tony Tell us another.
Arthur It's her gym ... she got body-builders 'n' all sorts of athletes coming here and she trains 'em ...
Phil I still say it's a bit much ...

Hazel goes up to Phil

Hazel That's for women.

Embarrassed reaction from Phil. The others laugh

Phil Obviously ...

Steve enters, late

Steve Oh yes, what is this ... luxury a-go-go?
Arthur Hazel, this is Steve ...
Steve Hazel ... nice to meet you ...
Hazel Hallo ...
Steve Do you have a nut in every bite ... ?
Hazel Humorous as well, isn't he ... ?
Steve Not funny but fast ...
Hazel OK then, warm-up on the bike ... let's make a start ... We'll start with a circuit ... Arthur ... legs, Frank sit-ups, Tony lats ... Phil bench ... we're looking——
Arthur I feel like I've shit my pants ...
Hazel I'm waiting ...
Arthur Sorry ...
Hazel We're looking for quick ten reps, make sure that the movement is strict, do not cheat ... if it's too light don't worry, it'll serve as a warm-up exercise, and go ...
Steve Hey, look at this ... I love it ... this is about my standard.

Each man begins to exercise ... The weights clunk about. Hazel watches. Steve fools ...

Hazel Concentrate on the movements ...
Steve Anybody want anything bringing from the shops ... ? "Riding along on a push-bike, honey ..." Ho ah ho ah ... (*He starts to make hand signals ... and banks the bike*) Get out of the way ...
Hazel Come on, cut it out ...
Steve Get out of the way ...

Hazel Very funny, now pack it in.

Hazel looks around the gym and sees all the lads on the machines, performing the exercises pathetically. She is very displeased

All right, change . . .

They all change. Arthur bangs the leg machine

Don't bang the weights.

The lads move to a different machine. Hazel gives them the go-ahead. They begin work on the machines. The effect is comic (and much improvising of the comic elements of the machines should be allowed) Hazel goes around to the various machines and encourages the lads to perform correctly. Tony is performing a neck-press with the weight to his head

Tony This one hurts your head.

Hazel encourages Frank on the hack-squat

Frank It's not very good for my piles.

Hazel gets them to change machines. A lighting change

Hazel (*sitting on the bike*) I worked them slowly to begin with. I could see that they were desperately out of shape——

All the lads perform one exercise

—and to give them their due, they played their part. We trained for a full week, split system, and Arthur would work at the back of the gym on ball skills.

The lads perform two repeats of the exercise

As we got into week three it was time to push them. (*To the players*) By the time we're finished you'll be doing thirty reps each.
All Thirty?

The players become more motivated and begin to count to themselves. Hazel is still encouraging their work. They count to thirty and as they count the volume increases, so by the time they reach thirty they are completely shouting

Black-out

ACT II

The players are still counting. Hazel walks around, encouraging them

Hazel Come on, pull ...!
Steve Get off.
Hazel No, pull ... good ...

Tony is on lats

    Pull ...
Tony I can't ... pull ...
Hazel Force it ... pull ... just your back ... good ...

Arthur is doing step-ups on the bench

    How many, Arthur?
Arthur Twenty ...
Hazel Another ... ten.
Arthur No, I'm knackered ... I want a rest ...
Hazel Another ten ... come on ... I'll count you ... one ... two ... three
    ... four ... five ... six ...
Arthur I'm gonna spew ...
Hazel Two more ... one ... two ... good ...
Arthur Oh shit ...

    Arthur dashes off-stage to be sick

Hazel Listen, lads ... listen ... a minute ... Phil, Tony. You've really got to
    go for it now, you've really got to push it ... push to the limits of the pain
    barrier ... otherwise the training's pointless.
Frank It's no good, I've had enough ...
Hazel You've got to go more, Frank ... hit the wall and straight out the
    other side ... that's what it's about fellers ...
Steve Can we just have a minute ... ?
Hazel OK, a timed minute ... starting now ...

They all relax. Hazel times them

Phil Do you get something sexual out of all this?
Hazel Don't talk shit ... forty seconds ...
Phil You're a sadist ... aren't you? Go on, admit it ...
Hazel Thirty seconds ...
Tony This is harder than pit work ...
Steve You're never there in any case ...
Tony I am when we're working ...
Hazel Fifteen ...

Frank Where's Arthur?
Hazel Being sick ... time, lads ... a minute ... back you get ...
Phil No, hang on ... have another minute ...
Hazel No come on ...
Tony Wait on a bit, Hazel ...
Hazel You said a minute ...
Phil Not a literal minute, a minute as in five minutes ...
Hazel Get back on these exercises, all of you ...
Steve No ... have a minute, man, for God's sake ...
Frank In a tick ...
Hazel Now ...
Phil We've been doing all the work ... it's easy to shout at people, I should
   know, I'm a teacher.
Hazel OK ... if you want to take that attitude, fair enough ...
Frank Thanks ...
Phil We'll train again in five or ten ...
Hazel When your muscle's have grown cold?
Tony Sarcasm ...
Steve The lowest form of ...
Hazel That's OK by me, it's your money, I suppose.
Tony Eh?

A beat

Steve You what?
Phil What is ... ?
Hazel All this training going to waste ... it's a waste of your money.
Tony Have we got to pay for all this?
Hazel No ... this is free ... the bet, I mean ...
Phil What are you on about ... ?
Steve What bet?
Hazel You're not that thick ... come on ...
Phil What's all this about a bet?
Hazel OK, forget it ... let's get back to work ...
Frank No ... hang on, I smell something a bit fishy ...
Steve I think it's Tony ...
Tony Bollocks you ...
Phil Is this summat to do with Arthur?
Hazel I really don't know.
Tony Come on, leave it ... it's got nothing to do with us ...

   Arthur enters

Arthur Jesus Christ ... I've just thrown half my insides up ... what's got
   nothing to do with you, Tony ... ?
Tony This bet ...
Arthur No ... right ... Come on, let's push on ...
Phil I want to know about this bet, Arthur ...
Frank Yeah, how does it affect us ... ?
Arthur Who told you?

Hazel I thought they knew ...

Arthur They do now ...

Steve What is it ... top secret or something?

Arthur Right ... I suppose I'd better tell you ...

Hazel I think you'd better ... before we go any further.

Arthur Sit down lads, this might hurt ...

Frank Us or you?

Arthur Both ...

They all sit down

So I told them about the bet ... and they were quite amiable about it ... Steve offered to put some money against them winning ...

Steve I'll have twenty quid against us Arth ...

Arthur We haven't got a chance, they said ... they were right ...

Tony We haven't got a chance ...

Arthur They didn't like Reg Welsh, that was clear ...

Steve He's a bastard ... and a crook ... take that from me ... I did his car once ... he never paid me ... sent two of his thugs around ...

Arthur That's the way Reg works ...

Frank It makes no difference anyway ... if we enter we might not get drawn against the Cobblers in any case ... we'll still probably go out in the first round.

Arthur I had to tell them it'd all been set up, that Reg had arranged for us to have a bye ... so we'd meet in the final ... that went down like a fart at a wedding ...

Tony You what?

Steve It's set up?

Arthur That's what I said ...

Phil Why us?

Tony Yeah ...

Frank We've never bloody won a game ...

Steve No ... never will ...

Phil Oh yeah ... I'm beginning to see it all ... you and Reg Welsh must have had a good laugh about us ... eh? Is that it? The Wheatsheaf ... the joke side ... the side who play with four men ... is that it?

Tony Right ... I'm not flogging my heart out for you to win three thousand ... not to be made a laughing stock ... for the likes of Reg Welsh ...

Arthur What have you got to lose ... ? It's my money ...

Frank It's your money, but it's our pride ... We've had enough jibes shoved down our throats without being set up against the best side in Yorkshire ... We want to win for a change ...

Arthur This is your chance ...

Phil Rubbish, that's utter rubbish and you know it. I'm off ... Come on, Steve ...

Steve I'm coming ...

Arthur Listen ...

Tony No ... you've got yourself in this shit ... you get yourself out of it ... don't get us involved ...

Frank So Reg Welsh thinks we're a joke team, does he . . . ?
Arthur Listen, Frank . . .
Frank Well that's fine by me . . . We are a bloody joke team . . . The game's off . . . You tell him . . . see if he finds it funny . . .

Frank leaves upstage, singing "Swing low, Sweet Chariot"

All the rest collect their belongings and leave

Hazel and Arthur are left

Hazel Sorry . . .
Arthur Ar . . .
Hazel I er . . .
Arthur Doesn't matter . . .
Hazel I thought they knew . . .
Arthur They had to know, I suppose . . .
Hazel Why didn't you tell them?
Arthur I wouldn't have got them this far . . . The mention of the Cobblers and legs turn to water . . .
Hazel Can you blame them?
Arthur No . . .
Hazel Well then . . . do you want a drink?
Arthur No . . . I feel physically and morally sick . . .
Hazel Have another word with them . . .
Arthur No . . .
Hazel Why?
Arthur Funny . . .
Hazel What?
Arthur I suppose Reg was right . . . said I'd seen too many *Rocky* films . . . where the underdog always wins . . .
Hazel It's nice to think about . . . nice ideal . . .
Arthur That's all it is . . . an ideal . . .
Hazel We need that sort of thing . . . to escape to . . .
Arthur Life's a bastard when you stop to think about it . . .
Hazel Nobody wins . . .
Arthur Ar well . . . that's my bank savings down the friggin' shoot.
Hazel He'll take the money, then?
Arthur Every last penny . . . plus the fact that I'll be the laughing stock . . .
Hazel So that's my part of the bargain wrapped up too, I suppose . . .
Arthur 'Fraid so . . .
Hazel Another icon shattered . . .
Arthur You what?
Hazel Broken dream . . .
Arthur Ar . . .
Hazel Oh well . . .
Arthur I'd like to be able to blame somebody . . . but I can't . . .
Hazel What are you going to do?
Arthur Ever heard of suicide . . . ?
Hazel Don't be stupid . . .

Arthur I think I'll just stay here for a bit ... if that's all right with you ...
Hazel Stay as long as you like ... I'm going to nip down to the bank.
Arthur Me too ...

Hazel exits

> Have you ever been out of your mind,
> And a scream of some kind ...
> Would be something obscene ...
> I feel like that now the day's at a close ...
> I knew that it wouldn't work out, I suppose ...
> And so as they all say ... to you, adieu and
> farewell ...
> ...and for the lies that I've told?
> I'll go rot in hell.

He gets up slowly and begins to leave

Tony comes into the gym and begins to train. Steve enters and gets on the bike. Frank and Phil follow and start their exercises

Phil Oi, fat bald bastard!
Arthur Eh!
Phil Get training, it's on ...
Arthur It's not ...
Tony It is ...
Steve So get moving ...
Frank Come on, Arthur, move it ...
Phil If we win we split the cash ... If we lose ... it's all yours ...
Arthur It's a deal ... and listen lads ... thanks.

Black-out

A spotlight picks out Hazel as she enters

Hazel The harder they trained the more single-minded they became, for the next three weeks they worked ... and strained and pained and planed the gained muscular power ... into shape, resilient and every hour ... they could, they knew they should, devote their time to the cause of winning. To the front page clause: "The Wheatsheaf beat the Cobblers out of Castleford." ... it was a tabloid dream, from a team that have schemed to pass and switch the ball, to play all fair and give the ground a swift turn of stud ... They would if they could, give the ball some air ... to turn defence to blunders with overlaps and scissor moves and lofty up 'n' unders of a genre not seen for years. Above all else, determined not to lose ... they chose to fight, though as you've seen upon this stage they've had the right for flight ... to withdraw ... let brass bands be heard and battle cries of awe ring from Hull to Featherstone ... And let our heroes know that they are not alone ... in their struggle to be kings on a paper throne ... Five weeks now gone ... The Wheatsheaf mean to see their form ... We see them now ... Still before the storm ...

*The Lights come up. The players are slowly finishing their exercises. They are
tired and drop to a resting place. Hazel walks around and gives them a towel.
They sit still and sweating ... quiet ... breathing heavily ... They remain
silent. Then:*

Phil Hey!

Arthur What?

Phil Do you want to hear a poem I've written about the game?

Tony No ...

Phil It's good listen ... It's a rip-off from Shakespeare ...

Steve Ronny Shakespeare used to do the washing for my Mam ...

Phil Prologue *Romeo and Juliet* ... it's taken from ...

Frank Very good ...

Phil Listen, you philistines ... you'll get this ... it's good:

> Two clubs each unlike in dignity,
> In fair Castleford where we'll lay our scene,
> A stupid bet, a bigotry ...
> A grim determination to win a match so keen ...

What do you reckon?

Tony Brilliant ...

Phil "Bigotry" doesn't really work ... but I couldn't think of another word.

Steve How about pillock?

Phil No ... it doesn't even work as a half-rhyme.

Tony Bloody hell!

Arthur Yeah.

Frank Knackered ...

Steve I feel drained ...

Hazel You've done well ... should be pleased with yourselves ... I'll put
the showers on ...

Hazel exits

Tony No shower for me ... straight down home.

Steve Early to bed ...

Phil Yeah ...

Arthur No ... not for me ...

Frank Why not?

Arthur I can't sleep unless I've had a drink ...

Phil You're in a bad way ...

Arthur If I don't have a couple of pints I just lay looking at the lampshade.

Steve I'll join you for a pint in the *Sheaf*, Arth ...

Arthur Right ... a couple of pints, fish and chips ... then up the wooden hill
to Bedfordshire ...

Frank Sounds like Tupper of the Track ...

Arthur Working-class hero ...

Frank True enough ...

Arthur Born with a silver knife in his back ...

Steve I feel right nervous ...

Tony I don't feel too bad ... I will do tomorrow ... I'll shit myself.

Steve Take some extra shorts, then.

A beat

Phil Arthur?
Arthur What?
Phil At the risk of sounding pedantic ...
All Whoooo ...!
Tony Get a big sign ... "Sage at work".
Phil All right, point taken.
Steve Brilliant.
Tony Oh yeah, brilliant ... brilliant ...
Arthur Go on ...
Phil I don't suppose you've overlooked the fact that we've still got only five players ...?
Arthur In the nineteen fourteen Rourke's Drift test Britain only had ten men ... and still beat a side of thirteen.
Phil That's little comfort.
Arthur Don't worry ...
Frank Have you got it in hand ... as they say ...?
Arthur I've made some arrangements ... Right, I'm down the showers and into the *Wheatsheaf* for a skinful ...
Phil Who's taking Steve and Frankie tomorrow?
Arthur Me ... I'll pick you up about half-ten, Frankie?
Frank Yeah ...
Arthur I'll make arrangements later, Steve ...
Steve Hang on, I'm coming ... See you in Castleford lads ...
All Right-oh ...
Frank Castleford here we come ...
Steve Frankie goes to Castleford ... eh hear that ...?
Tony Piss off ...
Steve Tony's good at one-liners.

Steve and Arthur leave, Steve singing "Relax"

Tony I don't think all this health food's been good for me.
Phil How come?
Tony I'm on the toilet all the time.
Frank It's good that, clear you out ...
Tony I don't know about that ... I feel like one long tube from mouth to arse.
Phil Oesophagus ...
Tony Oh ar ...

A beat

Phil How do you feel, Frank?
Frank OK ...
Phil Did you have a glance at those mags ...?
Frank Oh yeah ... very nice, very tasteful ... yeah ...
Phil Educational, aren't they?

Frank Yeah . . .

Phil I've got a couple of videos that might be worth a nod . . .

Frank Oh, right . . . tomorrow night, maybe . . . after the game?

Phil Let's see how it goes . . .

Tony How do you think we'll do?

Phil Dunno . . .

Frank I must admit that I think we look quite good . . .

Tony Depends who Arthur's bringing in . . .

Phil I've got a feeling that that might be another of Arthur's little foibles . . .

Frank Yeah . . . you might be right . . .

Tony Oh . . . If we lose, he's knackered.

Phil That's the price of gambling . . .

Tony Funny how you just do things, don't you . . . ? Make a decision to do something and then do it . . . That marathon . . . they do it just to say they've done it.

Phil Creativity, isn't it?

Tony Is it?

Phil Well, what would you have been doing if you hadn't been training . . . ?

Tony Arsing about, I suppose.

Phil Right . . . it's all part of the creative impulse . . . I tell the kids at school . . . creativity takes on many forms . . . They can't see it.

Frank Well, it's part of the health thing, isn't it . . . ? Life's like a tightrope . . . I read this in a book somewhere . . . never really forgotten it . . . life's a tightrope . . . we all travel in one direction, and if we don't surround ourselves with things to do . . . to help balance us . . . we fall off . . . something like that, anyway . . .

Phil I think I know what you mean.

Tony Do you think we ought to help Arthur out if we lose?

Frank In what way?

Tony With the money.

Phil We're not going to lose . . . no way am I having a woman make my back and legs and arms ache for five weeks to lose . . . no way . . . Shower, Frank . . . ?

Frank No . . .

Phil Tony . . . ?

Tony Can do . . .

Phil See you there . . .

Tony See you . . .

Hazel enters, carrying fresh towels

Phil See you tomorrow, Hazel . . . You'll be there, won't you?

Hazel Oh don't worry . . . I wouldn't miss it for the world . . .

Phil ⎫
Tony ⎭ (*together*) See you.

Tony and Phil exit

Hazel Aren't you going for a drink, Frank?

Frank No . . .

Hazel Oh ...

Frank I don't feel like it, to be honest ...

Hazel That's a shame ...

Frank I feel all melancholy.

Hazel Oh, what's brought that on?

Frank This game.

Hazel Oh ...

Frank When I was younger I used to play regularly ... Tina would bring the kids to watch ...

Hazel Aren't they coming tomorrow ... ?

Frank No ...

Hazel Oh ...

Frank We ... er ... we split up, you see ...

Hazel Oh, I'm sorry ...

Frank Took the kids ... I hardly see them now. They used to love to come and watch ... Carl and Peter ... two good props in the making ... Their mother'll be making them as soft as pudding.

Hazel That's mothers for you.

Frank Do you have any kids ... ?

Hazel No ...

Frank All this serious training, the lads as a team ... brought it all back to me ...

Hazel Yeah?

Frank I wasn't bothered when we were losing ... it didn't matter then, but we're in with a chance now ... I want them to be proud of me, do you know that ... ? I want them to be proud of me ... and she's making them as soft as shit ...

Hazel Go home, Frank ...

Frank Yeah ...

Hazel Save all the hatred for the field.

Frank You know what, Hazel?

Hazel No, what?

Frank Well, the lads and me were talking and we think that you're all right for a woman ...

Hazel Well that's very big of 'em, Frank ... very big of 'em ...

Frank I think that I will have that drink after all. Are you coming?

A beat

Hazel Well if I'm going to be one of the lads, I think I'd better.

They exit

The Lights cover to blue wash. All the gym equipment is removed save the two benches, which are placed side by side mid-stage. Brass music

Arthur enters and stands c

Hazel is downstage in a spotlight

Hazel So a steady drink for one and all, and then home to bed as the hour moved on apace. Our heroes bid each other adieu, and with confidence in their hearts they knew they stood a chance, a chance to win, to regain lost pride. They knew that fate was on their side.

Arthur I know it sounds funny but that night I prayed, I don't know why, I'm agnostic. Then I looked at my bank-book, placed it under Doreen's underwear in the bottom drawer, then I went to sleep.

The Lights fade on Arthur who exits

Phil enters, with a hot-water bottle, wearing a dressing-gown

Hazel Though Arthur slept in slumberland, in Phil's three-bedroomed semi his mind was filled with nightmarish thoughts and sleep he hadn't any.

The spot goes out on Hazel, who exits

Phil It's a very funny thing, when I was playing at Loughborough I never got nervous, I never had a thought about the game but tonight I'm like a bag of nerves . . . I've been to the toilet . . . back here to bed . . . I'm going to the toilet again in a minute . . . I'm sweating, sweat's dripping down my brow, even my palms are wet . . . I'll have to hope that I can, well . . . drift off to sleep.

The Lights change to a red wash covering the stage

And there I was, playing at Wembley in the Challenge Cup Final, playing for Fulham against the mighty Featherstone . . . There was hundreds and hundreds of bloated red faces looking down on me . . . I was on the wing and hundreds of yards away from the rest of the team. Featherstone looked massive . . . I gazed up and caught flashes of their kneecaps . . . They ran through to score, I glimpsed sight of hairs on the palms of their hands. We were losing . . . We needed a try. There was five minutes to play . . . There was an incident off the ball . . . "Gerroff me, you fat pig." I saw a gap, big as an ocean opening up in front of me . . . "Pass the ball . . . pass the ball!" And then it came out of a blur, the ball . . . God, I was nervous . . . I saw it coming towards me . . . daren't take my eye off it . . . I caught it and I ran . . . But I didn't move . . . I looked up . . . and the whole of Featherstone were coming towards me . . . men, women, children . . . miners, shop assistants, garage-owners . . . all on the field after me . . . so I ran . . . but the faster I ran the slower I went . . . I looked around for someone to pass to . . . but they were all having lunch . . . sat down having lunch in the middle of Wembley Stadium . . . "Go on, Phil," they said, "Go on . . . run mate, run" . . . and I was on the underground going down the Piccadilly Station, running and they were all running after me . . . Then a policeman stopped me and I tried to explain but he wanted my name and where I lived . . . I hit him . . . and ran . . . It was like running in a dream . . . jumping over buildings and landing at different places . . . but wherever I landed they were still there, coming around the corner . . . I ran up an alleyway . . . I was cornered . . . I looked around at them . . . trapped, so I ran towards them . . . I just closed my eyes and ran . . .

Phil exits

A bluish-coloured wash covers the stage, quite dimly

Arthur, Tony, Frank and Steve move about in the lights, growling and making large movements. They are the Cobblers team. They arrange the benches so they're like they were at the beginning of Act I. The players sit down. On the backs of their shirts they have "Cobblers Arms" emblazoned. They wear full rugby regalia—the players will play the parts of both teams. The Lights come up

Arthur Somebody's gonna get smacked ...
Tony Yeah ...
Frank I'm gonna kill somebody.
Tony Yeah, kill!
Steve Hurt their bodies ...
Arthur Somebody's gonna get their neck broke and their body hurt.
Tony Yeah ... and hurt ...
Frank What are we?
All Mean.
Frank What do we want?
All We want to win.
Frank What will we do?
All We'll kill to win.
Frank Who are we gonna kill?
All The Wheatsheaf wallies.
Frank Why?
All 'Cos we hate the bastards ...
Arthur (*shaking his fist*) Somebody's gonna get some of this ... !
Tony Keep the ball tight ... until we've made the overlap ...
Steve Don't switch it, then ...
Arthur Run straight at 'em ... Run till you can see the whites of their eyes, and when you can see the whites ... stick an arm straight in 'em ...
Frank Right, here we go ...
Arthur Put the willies up 'em ...

They sing a war-like chant, with a slapping of thighs and a banging of feet on the floor. This gets louder and louder, ending in screams and growls

Black-out

The Lights come up to reveal the same players, but very quiet (in total contrast) and sitting down. They have just heard what the Cobblers have done

Steve Hear that?
Tony Yeah.
Steve Jesus Christ, I'm shitting it ...
Arthur Ar ...
Frank I think they mean business ...
Tony Do they know that we've had a bye on purpose?
Arthur Yeah ...
Tony They are not going to be too happy about that, are they?
Arthur No ...
Steve Have they got seven men ... ?

Frank And two subs ... I watched them play the first round.

Tony Yeah, the subs are like whippets ...

Steve They would be ...

Arthur Remember what I've said all along ... don't let your nerves get the better of you. Stick to the plans ...

Tony Where's Phil ... ?

Phil enters, walking as if he's got the shits—which he has

Phil Have you seen the size of that lot?

Steve Where've you been, man ... ?

Phil Toilet ...

Tony Trying to escape ...

Phil I'm loose.

Frank We'll all be loose by the time we've finished this ...

Phil They have got some big lads.

Arthur Yeah ... and they've brought a couple of ringers in.

Tony He wants his money, doesn't he?

Arthur He's not gonna get it, though ... over my dead body ...

Steve Hey, steady on, Arthur, I'll play but I'm not going that far.

Tony How long is there?

Arthur Five minutes ...

Frank Let them go out first ...

Phil They're out ... I could hear them changing when I was on the toilet ... the seat was vibrating.

Steve What's the weather like ... ?

Phil Not bad ... good for running.

Arthur Keep it wide ... don't let them keep it tight ...

Tony Wide ... right ...

Steve Oh, before I forget, Arthur ... nice one on the kit ...

Frank Oh yeah ... good stuff, mate.

Tony Yeah ...

Arthur I know this is the wrong time to say this, lads ... but I had to fork out a fiver each for the hire of the kit ... if at some time in the not too distant future ...

Phil Did I have a dream last night?

Steve And me ... I was playing at Wembley.

Phil looks at him

Frank I know what you mean, I was playing all last night.

Arthur Remember the set moves when you get a call ... move it, right?

All Right.

Steve Arthur, I suppose these ringers you were talking about were just figments of your imagination, they're not going to appear, are they?

A beat

Arthur Ar well ... it's a very long and complicated story.

A beat

All Ay, it would be.

Hazel enters, wearing the same kit. Music plays

All the players look together as a team at Arthur

Steve You're not serious?
Frank Is this the arrangement? I mean, she might get hurt.
Hazel Well, what did you expect?
Phil Does she know the moves? I mean, I'm not being rotten, Hazel, just . . . well you know?
Arthur Where do you think I got the idea from?
Frank He is not thick.
Steve No, we are.
Tony Well, if you play as good as you train . . . it's OK by me . . .
Steve And me.
Phil And me.
Hazel Right, thanks team . . .
Tony I feel a bit emotional . . .
Frank Let's get out there . . .
Arthur Yeah . . .
Tony Having a woman playing . . . I love it, aarrhhh!
Phil It will probably throw 'em.
Steve It's thrown me.
Arthur Well, let's just say . . . all the best . . .
Frank All the best, Arth . . .
Tony Good luck.
Arthur And you.
Phil It's a ridiculous thing to do, Arthur . . . but thanks . . .
Hazel If you don't live life to the full, what's the point?
Phil Here we go, then . . .

They all prepare. There is a sudden air of complete seriousness. They shake and concentrate . . . and then . . . out into the stage space they run . . . They jump up and down in the stage space . . . Arthur steps forward . . . and shakes hands with "Frank" of the Cobblers

Arthur Hope it'll be a good game.
"Frank" You're going to die.
Arthur Don't be like that.
"Frank" You're in a box.
Hazel Which way are we playing, Arthur?
Arthur Our kick-off.
Tony What's their captain like?
Arthur I think he must have trouble at home.
Steve How come?
Arthur He's not a happy man.
Phil Oh . . .
Arthur I don't think that they like us very much . . .
Steve Funny, that . . . they look a friendly bunch . . .

Tony Has anybody seen *Flesh-eating Zombies*?
Frank I know what you're saying ...
Phil I don't like the look of mine ...
Arthur Man for man marking ...
Tony I'll have yours, then ...
Phil Right, fill out the space ... all the area ...

The players move into the space

Steve They are massive ...
Phil I bet they can't run ...
Steve Half of 'em can't talk ... (*He mimics a gross beast*)
Hazel They've got legs like tree-trunks and shoulders like they'd swallowed
  two dustbins ... They hate us ... you can see it ...
Frank Why do the opposition always look so big?
Tony I bet they've only got four teeth between 'em ...
Phil Watch for the funny switch ... up on 'em quick ...
Tony Once the first tackle's been made I'll be OK ...
Steve I'm like a jelly-fish ...
Hazel How do you think I feel?

A beat

Frank Straight on 'em, a man each ...
Arthur Anybody ever seen *Zulu*?
Tony He's off ...
Steve You ought to be on "Film Eighty-four".
Arthur It reminds me of *Zulu* ... Rourke's Drift ... we're the British ...
  they're the ...
Phil Warriors ... millions of 'em, all stood on the cliffs, I've seen it ...
Frank Looks like it ... and all ...
Phil Yeah ... they all got killed ...
Arthur They got VCs though ...
Tony I'll be Michael Caine ...
Steve Aren't we having a team photo, Arthur ...
Arthur We'll have it later ...
Steve In hospital?

A whistle is blown

Hazel Arthur kicked off a large rambling grubber kick along the ground ...
  The sound of leather on leather was sickening, even from the kick-off ...
Tony Nobbler Knowles ...
Phil For the Cobblers caught the ball ...
Steve Their most feared forward ...

*Arthur during this time has held off a ball. Frank positions himself so that the
back of his shirt shows the Cobbler's insignia—he is therefore now Nobbler
Knowles. "Frank" takes the ball at pace, and despite desperate tackles from
the Wheatsheaf players he scores a try downstage-centre. He turns round and
becomes Frank again. Dejection amongst the Wheatsheaf side. They retrieve
the ball*

Phil Steve ... tackle!
Steve Tackle that?
Phil Yeah ...
Steve I didn't see you making much effort ...
Phil I was covering ...
Steve I was covering ...
Tony Your eyes, eh?
Hazel Good start, lads ...
Frank What about the conversion ... ?
Phil They'll not bother ... They know that they've won.
Arthur Right, come on ... let's see nobody chickening out, right?

Arthur, Hazel, Phil and Steve move sideways across the stage, covering the Cobblers

Our kick ...
Hazel Arthur kicked a nice long one, which bounced inside their twenty-two metres line ...
Steve For God's sake, watch that big 'un ...

Arthur passes the ball to "Frank" (Nobbler), who runs and is challenged by Steve and Phil, but manages to pass to "Tony" (Stabber), who tries to get around Arthur and does, but is caught by the shirt by Hazel. She tries to push him back, but he runs to score another try for the Cobblers

Hazel Sorry, lads ... I had him ...
Tony Eight-nil ... in two minutes ...
Steve It's all over, lads ...
Tony You said it ...
Steve All over ...
Tony Oh shite ...
Arthur Come on ... get it together ... they're only flesh and blood ...
  Think about the game ... Come on! ... ! (*Shouting*) Long kick, Phil ...
  (*Whispering*) Short one ...
"Tony" Watch out for the long one ...

Arthur rolls the ball on-stage. Phil runs forward and picks up the ball. "Tony" (Stabber) is over him and won't let him play the ball

Play the ball ...
Phil In a tick ...
"Tony" Play the ball ...
Phil Let me get up, then ...
"Tony" Play the ball ... !
Phil Hang on ...
"Tony" Play it ... !
Phil All right ... no need to get physical ...

A push from "Tony"

Steady on ... it's only a game ...
"Tony" Come on then, short-arse ...

Another push from "Tony"

Phil Look, will you pack that in?
Steve Send him to the back of the class, Phil . . .
"Tony" Play the ball . . .

Phil plays the ball to Hazel, who passes to Arthur, who passes to Steve. Steve is hit by "Frank" (Nobbler) in the cobblers and falls in agony to the floor. He writhes for a while

Steve Oh . . . !
Phil Come on, Steve, play the ball . . .
"Frank" Play the ball . . .
Steve Oh . . . oh . . . oh . . . my goolies . . . I'm ruined . . . I'm finished . . .
"Frank" Play the ball . . .
Arthur Count 'em . . .
Phil He's only got one . . .
Hazel Fourth tackle coming up . . .

Steve gets up. Tony comes to watch him. "Frank" becomes Frank. Steve plays the ball to Hazel who plays a blind-side ball to Frank, who takes it and growls his way to C

Hazel Go on, Frank.
Steve Leg it, Frankie . . .

Frank begins to move but is brought down by "Tony" (Stabber). "Tony" stands over Frank in the same manner as before

"Tony" Play the ball . . .
Frank Hang on a minute, man . . .
"Tony" Play the ball . . . !
Frank Hang on . . .
"Tony" Play it . . . !

In slow motion Frank grabs "Tony" by the shirt, brings his head back and nuts him full in the face. The reaction is given from the rest of the players who make the sound effects. "Tony" goes down and bounces off the floor

Phil Nice, Frank . . .
Frank (*to the Referee*) I think he's got something in his eye, Ref.

Frank plays the ball to Hazel, to Arthur, to Steve (who is struggling after the kick in the goolies)

Steve Not to me . . . I can't move . . . (*Steve passes the ball to Phil*)
Phil I found some space on the left, even if it meant running around the back of our line . . . I put my head down and ran . . .
Arthur Go on, Phil . . .
Hazel Nice, Phil . . .
Frank Lovely man . . . go on, yer . . .
Phil A man to beat . . .

"Tony" tackles but Phil breaks free. He scores in the corner. He and the rest of the team are elated

A try ... a try in the corner ... !
Steve I don't believe it ...
Tony Whooh ... !

Shouts of delight all round

Frank Brilliant ... !
Arthur Great solo effort, lads ... great solo effort ... well played lads.
Phil (*breathless*) Thanks ...
Hazel Eight-four ...
Arthur Come on, we can beat these ...
Hazel One flukey try ...
Arthur We can hammer this lot ...
Phil Hey, look at 'em, they don't believe it ...

Phil makes a "V" sign at the audience

Tony Come on, keep it going ...

Hazel stands C. *The rest of the players are at the back of the stage. Hazel picks up the ball. The rest prepare to work a move*

Hazel You could see that they didn't like it ... It was eight-four, with three minutes of the first half left to play. Their kick to us a long one right down to the touch in goal area ... I picked it up and they were on us like growling bears ...
Steve Hazel ... !
Hazel I saw Steve coming inside, calling out ...
Steve Here ... give it ...

Steve receives the ball and begins to run DL. *Tony comes from* UL *and takes the ball on a scissor movement. Tony has the ball* C *and delivers a reverse pass to Phil, who gives a quick ball to Frank, who finds Arthur. Arthur takes the ball on downstage and performs a dummy* DR, *and moves* C. *(This movement must be done at speed in order to get the slow-motion effect later.) Arthur stands* C

Arthur And I'm there in the clear with about ten yards to go ... and there it is, another try ... beneath the sticks a captain's try ... yes, what a marvellous equalising try from Billy Boston.

Arthur dives. The players celebrate and lift Arthur aloft

Tony Half-time.
Phil Eight-all.
All Eight all eight all eight all eight all.

Arthur drops his shorts, baring his bum to the Cobblers

Steve Up yours, Reg Welsh.

A change of colour wash to blue for voice-over action replay

Voice-over (*in an Eddie Waring accent*) Now let's just have a look at that try once again ... let's see how it all started, Alex ... Cobblers kick long and it's collected by Scott ... formerly of Hunslett ... and moved swiftly ...

out to Steve Edwards, who's a little slow for a big fellow really, Alex . . . to
Burtoft who does well, and then this man Hopley, formerly of London . . .
and the England Colts . . . and a fine runner with the ball to Rowley,
looking tired and drawn . . . and a captain's try, Alex, for Arthur Hoyle,
formerly of Wakefield . . . so as we go into the break it's even stevens . . .

*Throughout the recent commentary the players have been re-running the whole
of the last try sequence. (If the players are of a standard and the space permits,
then sundry other moves can well be improvised.) At the completion of the re-
run the players sit down, breathless, in the middle of the field. It is indeed half-
time*

Steve Eight-all . . .
Phil It would have been ten-eight if we'd have bothered with the conver-
sion . . .
Tony Forget that . . . we can score tries . . . just keep the ball away from
them big 'uns . . .
Steve Anybody got any beer?
Frank I've got a feeling that they're gonna get nasty this next half . . .
Phil Yeah, watch that number eight . . .
Frank I'll have him . . .
Hazel Poke his eyes out . . . he scratched me . . .
Arthur Hazel . . . you're doing well . . .
Tony Yeah . . . not bad . . .
Phil They're trying to keep it tight . . .
Arthur Keep tackling up, man and ball . . . I think we've thrown 'em . . .
Phil We're doing all right . . .
Steve We're doing brilliant . . .
Arthur Keep it on this half these ten minutes . . . think about it . . . when you
go in go in and mean it . . . look for the blind side moves . . . let's see some
flair . . . see some ball play . . .
Tony I'll tell you what . . . the crowd are loving this . . . I can hear Gayle
shouting a mile away . . .
Steve Can I have my share of the brass now Arth?
Arthur Don't speak too soon . . .
Phil Look at 'em . . . bringing two subs on . . . ringers . . .
Arthur Bastards . . .
Frank Do you know 'em?
Arthur One of them was a Warrington winger . . .
Tony Wonder what they're saying . . .

Black-out. Gruff, fierce voices of the Cobblers team are heard

"Frank" Get that bald head and smash it . . .
"Arthur" Yeah . . .
"Phil" Throw the ball about to the wings more . . .
"Steve" Try and stretch 'em . . .
"Frank" Yeah, stretch 'em . . .
"Tony" Start putting it together . . . They've come at us . . . Let's start
getting back at them . . .

"Arthur" Above all make every tackle hurt ... Let them know that they've
   been in a game.
"Frank" And hurt 'em ...

The Lights come back up on the Wheatsheaf team

Phil Right, we're ready ...
Arthur Hey, I've just had a thought ...
Frank What?
Arthur Wait here ... shan't be a minute ...

   Arthur exits

Steve Where's he going?
Tony Probably had a brain-wave ...
Hazel I've got a feeling that this is going to be a long ten minutes ...
Phil Listen, Hazel, when you get a break, when you see a gap, go for it ...
   you're being predictable.
Hazel Right ...

   Arthur returns with six gum-shields

Arthur Here ... wear these ... I'd forgotten about 'em ... If it's going to get
   rough ... it might save a few teeth for someone ...

*They all fit their gum-shields. All the players go out onto the pitch. They
attempt to talk to each other, but no-one can understand what the others are
saying. In response to every remark there is a misunderstanding nod. The
image should be funny ... until ...*

Steve I'm not wearing this, Arthur ...
Frank Nor me ...
Arthur Stick it down your sock in that case ...

Some stick it down their socks. Some merely throw them to the side

   So at eight-all we had a chance ...
Phil But the Cobblers were no duck eggs ...
Frank They came back at us with open rugby ...
Steve And by one minute into the second half ...
Tony They had scored two remarkable tries ...
Frank Which they converted ...
Hazel The score was twenty points to eight ...
Arthur We started to swing the ball about ...
Frank Gave it some air ...
Tony Every opening we saw we went for with close support ...
Phil With overlaps ... and quick switching of the ball ...
Steve Tony scored ... under the posts ...
Hazel Arthur converted and the score was twenty-fourteen ...
Arthur Scrum down ...

*The front row is down. Hazel has the ball. They prepare to go into the scrum
position. As they go down there is much growling and biting of ears*

Frank Come here, I'll bite your neck off . . .

Hazel puts the ball into the scrummage. Arthur hooks. Hazel takes the ball and works a scissors with Phil, who runs into the front row. He is brought down with a sickening thud. He gets up and pushes the tackler in the chest. There ensues a series of pushing involving all the players. The word they use is "Yeah": hence "Yeah", "Yeah", "Come on", "Yeah", until a rather nasty scene of fighting breaks out. Arthur has eventually to be held back by the rest of the players as he threatens the audience

Arthur Right, hit me . . . just hit me, let's see what that'll prove . . . yeah, you chickens . . . I'd take you all on . . . all of you.

Phil Leave it, Arthur . . .

Arthur Don't like it, do you . . . Come on, play the ball, we've got these . . .

Tony I got the ball inside their twenty-two . . .

Hazel And quick as a flash . . .

Frank Tony had scored a drop-kick . . .

They all cheer

Steve One point for that . . . pathetic rules . . .

Hazel Twenty points to fifteen . . .

Arthur How long left, Ref?

Phil Two minutes . . .

Frank Don't let them in our half . . .

Steve For those two minutes the Cobblers threw everything they had at us . . . It was man to man tackling all the way, now.

Three players are the Cobblers and three the Wheatsheaf. Throughout this it's a tackle on a man each. As they pass the ball from player to player Steve intercepts and waves the ball at the audience

Steve I got the ball from a Cobbler's mistake . . .

Steve gets the ball and weaves in and out of the rest of the players. Hazel stays upstage and Steve passes the ball to her. The rest of the team stand DR in pairs ready to catch Steve. Steve gives and gets the ball from Hazel. He runs towards the four Cobblers players and jumps into their arms. He makes two attempts to play the ball over the line. On the third he succeeds, and is held aloft by the four, who are now the Wheatsheaf team. Exaltation abounds

A try . . . a try . . . right in the corner . . .

Phil Why didn't you go under the sticks?

Steve A try . . . in the corner . . .

They all congratulate Steve

Tony It was a long kick . . . I took it . . . but the angle was too acute . . .

Tony mimes the ball going toward the posts. In the event it misses, and the players illustrate their dismay

Bastard . . . sorry, lads . . .

Hazel Twenty-nineteen.

Arthur One minute left.
Frank Watch the time-wasting, Ref.
Phil Watch the kick . . .

The players are all standing upstage, Frank has the ball behind his back. The line-up across the stage reads: Frank, Phil, Arthur, Tony, Steve, Hazel

Steve As soon as you get it, attack . . .
Arthur Fifty seconds . . .
Tony Get it kicked, man . . . Ref, that's time-wasting . . .
Arthur They kicked . . . it was long . . . but I expected that . . .

Frank tosses the ball from behind his back to Phil during the next sequence of dialogue. The ball goes all the way down the line to Hazel, who passes back inside to Steve. Phil has dropped back-stage. Tony, Arthur and Frank have become the Cobblers c

Phil I stayed back and set off on a long run . . .
Frank Close support was needed . . .
Steve Up and under . . . !

Steve has the ball. He hoists the ball with a boot. Hazel takes it from behind his back. Phil runs and is hoisted into the air by Cobblers ("Frank", "Tony" and "Arthur"). Hazel tosses the ball to Phil and "Frank" (Nobbler) hits him in the mouth. They all fall to the ground. Hazel blows the whistle. All are on the floor. Phil holds his mouth

All Penalty, Ref . . . !
Steve I'll take it.
Hazel Let me take it.
Tony I'll take it.
Frank Let Phil take it . . .
Steve Let Tony have a go . . .
Arthur I'll take it . . .
Frank Don't miss . . .
Hazel Twenty seconds left . . . This would be the last kick of the game . . .
Arthur I could kick this in my slippers . . .
Phil Take your time . . .
Tony Don't hook it . . .
Arthur I know it's a straight-forward kick . . .
Hazel Arthur carefully placed the ball . . .
Tony Considered its oval shape . . .
Phil Wiped the mud from his boot . . .
Steve Stood slowly upright . . .
Frank Stepped back majestically . . .
Phil Raised his head . . .
Steve And struck the ball beautifully . . .
Hazel We looked up to see the ball soar . . . into the air . . .
Phil High, very high . . .
Steve We watched the ball . . .
Tony As it . . . ?

Arthur Struck the post . . .
Frank And bounced back towards us . . .

All the players mouth "Fucking hell" as they see defeat. A whistle is blown

Tony Full time.
Arthur Shit . . . shit . . . shit . . .

Arthur falls to the floor: "Jesus Christ". The other players are stunned. There is a moment's silence

   Don't anybody talk to me.
Tony What're you going to do, Arthur?
Arthur Kill myself . . .

The rest of the team sit about

Phil I'm off . . .
Tony Where?
Phil Get changed.

Both go and stand UC, *with their backs to the audience, holding hands as the Cobblers*

Steve Whoooh, eh? Twenty-bloody-nineteen . . .
Frank We had 'em worried, though . . .
"Phil" ⎱
"Tony" ⎰ *(together)* Well played Cobblers.

Steve and Frank get a bench each and sit on it. The Lights fade to interior

Hazel I didn't know what to do or what to say . . . They seemed to have nothing left . . . nothing left to give . . . We all crept silently back to the dressing-room and sat . . .

Arthur is still left on-stage, crying, but the location has changed to the dressing-room. The players sit and remain silent for a long, long time. They begin to take off their shoes, socks, shirts, etc.

Tony Rocky didn't cry, Arthur . . .
Arthur I know . . .
Tony Yeah . . .
Arthur *Rocky's* a bleeding film . . .
Tony I know . . .
Frank Oh, well . . .

A number of cans of beer are intermittently pulled open

Steve Well, we can't all be Rocky Balboa, but . . . ?
Phil At least we tried . . .
Frank "Pack up all my cares and woe . . . here I go, singing low . . ."
Arthur We didn't finish the marathon, though, did we . . . ?
Frank "Bye bye blackbird . . ."
Arthur Sorry, lads . . . I've let you down . . .
Steve Don't worry, Arthur . . . we'll beat 'em next time . . .
Arthur You what?

Frank "Where somebody waits for me ..."

Steve Next time we play 'em ... the bastards, I got a right crack on my
   ear ...

Frank "Sugar's sweet, so is she ..."

Arthur No ... there's no next time ...

Frank "Bye bye blackbird ..."

Tony What about the five weeks' trial ...?

Phil Yeah, you've passed ... coach for life ...

Hazel Another challenge, Arthur ...

Arthur No ...

Phil Listen you stay with us ... you and us lot ... we're a good team ...

Frank "No-one here can love or understand me, oh what hard-luck stories
   they all hand me ..."

Phil A great team.

Steve One lousy point ...

Frank There's worse things happen in the world ...

Arthur As my Dad always said, there's always another day ...

Phil Very true ...

Arthur I suppose that ... oh no ...

Frank Go on ...

Steve Suppose what?

Arthur I've got this daft idea that we go over to Reg Welsh ... right ... ?
   Double or nothing ...

Phil And they field no ringers?

Arthur Exactly ...

Tony That's six grand ... Shit ... This could go on for ever ...

Frank But next time we'll win ...

Steve I'm in for that ... Let's show these bastards ...

Phil I thought this was your last game?

Steve It was ...

Frank Just one point ...

Arthur What?

Frank We find a kicker ...

Hazel I can goal kick ...

Tony Why didn't you say owt?

Hazel Nobody asked me ...

Arthur So ...

Steve So what?

Arthur Is it on ... ?

Steve ⎫ (*together*) You bet ...
Hazel ⎭   I'm in.

Tony ⎫ (*together*) It's on ...
Phil ⎭   Let's kill 'em ...

Arthur What if Reg won't accept the bet?

All Oh yeah ...

*Frank begins to sing once more. Slowly they all begin to join in the song of
"Bye bye blackbird". Arthur is the last one to join in. As they reach the end of*

the second verse they are transformed. "Rocky" theme music plays, and slowly they all stand. Each character is introduced over a loud speaker and the name of the actor given, like at the end of "Dallas" or a similar soap opera. As the credits are given the actors play selected parts of the play: Tony's try, Steve's try, Hazel's exercises, Frank's head butt. Phil is the last one, with a smack in the mouth. All the players raise a hand to the audience, give a knowing smile that "Up 'n' Under Two" is coming and take their bows ...

CURTAIN

FURNITURE AND PROPERTY LIST

ACT I

On stage: Sit-ups rack
Hooks. *On one:* rugby shirt
Bench. *On it:* rugby ball

Off stage: Kit bag with kit **(Tony)**
Kit bag with kit **(Phil)**
Kit bag with kit and massive rugby shirt **(Frank)**
Kit bag **(Steve)**
Rugby ball **(Stage management)**
Beers **(Frank, Phil)**
Rugby balls **(Arthur)**
Lat machine, exercise bike, bench press, hack-squat, sit-ups bench, step-up bench **(Players)**

Personal: **Reg:** pack of cigars
Arthur: money in pocket
Hazel: wrist-watch

ACT II

On stage: As end Act I

Off stage: Towel **(Hazel)**
Fresh towels **(Hazel)**
Hot-water bottle **(Phil)**
Ball **(Players)**
6 gum shields **(Arthur)**
Cans of beer **(Players)**

Personal: **Hazel:** whistle

LIGHTING PLOT

Property fittings required: nil

A bare stage

ACT I

To open: General lighting

Cue 1	**Frank:** "... pledge their gold ..." *Fade upstage lighting*	(Page 1)
Cue 2	**Hazel** exits *Bring up lights upstage on* **Frank, Tony** *and* **Phil** *in dressing-room*	(Page 5)
Cue 3	**Steve, Frank, Phil** *and* **Tony** DS and find a space *Cross-fade to exterior lighting* DS	(Page 8)
Cue 4	**Arthur:** "Our lass'll kill me ..." *Black-out*	(Page 12)
Cue 5	**Reg** enters *Light on him*	(Page 12)
Cue 6	**Reg:** "... 'who's bet all he's got.' " *General lighting*	(Page 12)
Cue 7	**Reg** exits *Cut light on him*	(Page 13)
Cue 8	**Hazel:** "The rest were supping ale ..." *Cross-fade to* **Frank** *and* **Phil**	(Page 13)
Cue 9	**Frank** and **Phil** both sigh ... drink their beer *Cross-fade to* **Arthur**	(Page 14)
Cue 10	**Arthur:** "... waiting and waiting." *Cross-fade to* **Frank** *and* **Phil**	(Page 14)
Cue 11	**Phil:** "Cheers." *Cross-fade to* **Hazel**	(Page 15)
Cue 12	**Hazel:** "... subjects he held dear." *Cross-fade to* **Arthur**	(Page 15)
Cue 13	**Arthur:** "... shouting and all." *Cross-fade to* **Hazel** *and increase lighting*	(Page 15)
Cue 14	**Arthur** exits *Fade lights*	(Page 16)
Cue 15	**Steve** comes on *Bring up lighting*	(Page 16)

Cue 16	**Arthur** goes *Increase lighting*	(Page 17)
Cue 17	**Steve:** "... into my shorts once." *Black-out; then overhead light on* **Arthur**	(Page 21)
Cue 18	**Arthur:** "... I lay awake ..." *Bring up general lighting*	(Page 21)
Cue 19	**Frank:** "And me ..." *Change to gymnasium lighting*	(Page 22)
Cue 20	**Frank:** "... for my piles." **Hazel** gets them to change machines *Lighting change*	(Page 24)
Cue 21	Players reach thirty, shouting *Black-out*	(Page 24)

ACT II

To open: General gymnasium lighting

Cue 22	**Arthur:** "... listen, lads ... thanks." *Black-out, then spot on* **Hazel**	(Page 29)
Cue 23	**Hazel:** "... Still before the storm ..." *Gymnasium lighting*	(Page 30)
Cue 24	**Hazel** and **Frank** exit *Lights cover to blue wash*	(Page 33)
Cue 25	When ready *Light on* **Arthur** C, *spot on* **Hazel** DS	(Page 33)
Cue 26	**Arthur:** "... then I went to sleep." *Fade light on* **Arthur**	(Page 34)
Cue 27	**Hazel:** "... he hadn't any." *Fade spot on* **Hazel**	(Page 34)
Cue 28	**Phil:** "... drift off to sleep." *Change to red wash covering stage*	(Page 34)
Cue 29	**Phil:** "... closed my eyes and ran ..." *Change to dim bluish wash*	(Page 34)
Cue 30	Cobblers team sit down *General lighting*	(Page 35)
Cue 31	Cobblers sing war-like chant, ending in screams and growls *Black-out; then bring up general lighting*	(Page 35)
Cue 32	**Steve:** "Up yours, Reg Welsh." *Change to bluish wash*	(Page 41)
Cue 33	**Voice-over:** "... it's even stevens ..." *Return to general lighting*	(Page 42)
Cue 34	**Tony:** "Wonder what they're saying ..." *Black-out*	(Page 42)

Cue 35   **Frank:** "And hurt 'em."   (Page 43)
            General lighting

Cue 36   **Steve** and **Frank** get a bench each and sit down   (Page 46)
            Change to interior lighting

Cue 37   As *Rocky* theme music plays   (Page 48)
            Increase lighting

EFFECTS PLOT

ACT I

MADE AND PRINTED IN GREAT BRITAIN BY
LATIMER TREND & COMPANY LTD PLYMOUTH

MADE IN ENGLAND